Living with Wieners …

and guys, too

By Judy S. Watts

With love, devotion and gratitude to my long-suffering husband Pat "The Hubster" Watts, our incredible children Sean (Surfer Dude) and Paul (Manchild #2) for their support and good humor in allowing me to share our lives with readers over these many years. A special nod goes to the wee dachshunds that have added the background noise to our lives. They are always happy to see whichever one of us walks in the door.

It all started with SAM – Sean's August Moon – bought for Surfer Dude for his 10th birthday. Sam was the man, the first weenie dog to own us. Since then we've welcomed Princess Sally, Sweet Charlotte, Mabel the roadside rescue, Cassie the upstate rescue and Penny the abandoned backyard beauty.

The stories that follow were published over the lifetimes of some of our weenies.

For those who love little dogs – or dogs of any stature – I hope our family dog stories will bring a smile to your face and a memory to your heart.

Judy Stein Watts
7/21/13

Table of Contents

Pets beg question, 'Who owns whom?'

For man-child #1's tenth birthday, we presented him with Sam. Sam's a trip.

Sam has his own life going on.

Sam basically owns us. If he could drive the convertible to the pet store to buy his own kibble or jump onto the couch without a boost, he really wouldn't need us.

The difference between him and us is that he doesn't waste his time working, going to school or maintaining a home.

We do that for him.

We also have turtles. Five to be exact. They were all rescued from highways and byways. They live in our back yard in a fenced-off area that includes their own little pond.

They also don't work.

But they also don't bark.

The only discernible work they do is each digging a hole

in the late fall. They climb into their respective holes for a six-month siesta. Since they sleep half their lives, I don't have to feed them all winter – making them the world's most perfect pets.

They do occasionally fight each other over a mushroom, but that's about as excited as they get.

Der Wiener, however, gets charged up about everything.

Sam might be our pet, but not to be outdone, Sam acquired his own pet.

We discovered this one afternoon as the Hubster and I sat on the back patio enjoying a quiet spring afternoon.

Sam lurched about after the squirrels that taunted him. They'd get just out of his short reach, then scurry up nearby trees.

Sam's very short. (His reach extends an elaborate 18 inches if he stretches as tall as he can).

Anyway. We sat there enjoying a few adult refreshments when Sam suddenly went nuts, barking like Hitler on speed. He was out near the back of the lot about 50 feet from where we sat. We watched for a few minutes as the barking – focused at something on the ground – got worse. He went round and round screeching, barking, yelping. Yodeling.

"Whatya' suppose he's up to this time?" the Hubster

asked.

"Can't imagine," I replied munching on another Frito.

But I was curious.

We weren't too alarmed at first because Sam has a penchant for going crazy in short bursts. Usually, after a couple of minutes, he gets tired of whatever got him going in the first place and walks away.

Not this time.

"He's getting worse," I said after a while. He'd barked and worked his short little self into a flying duck fit for about 10 minutes by then. Since his attention span equals that of the average 2-year-old's, I figured it was time for the Hubster to check it out.

"You don't suppose he's onto a snake, do you?" I asked.

"Maybe," my hero said heading for the garage.

The Hubster emerged with a hoe and headed for the source of all the commotion. The dog was now more hysterical than a 14-year-old girl freshly spurned by her boyfriend of three days.

Anyway, my beloved stood out there, hoe in hand, (like half the duo in the painting "American Gothic") for about five minutes watching weenie-pet revolve frantically around the new center of his universe.

I sat poised to hop on the nearest high thing should the object of Sam's attention turn out to be something that slithers.

After a while, my beloved ambled back to his lounge chair, tossed the hoe to the ground and shook his head.

"What is it?" I asked. "What's he got?"

The Hubster looked me right in the eye and said, "A brick."

"What do you mean, 'a brick?'" I asked.

"A brick," he said again, looking at me and then back toward our berserk canine.

"I don't understand," I said.

With that he turned, took my hand and said, "He's barking at a brick, Judy. A half of a brick – like the house is made of bricks."

Seriously?

I went to see for myself.

And there he was, sure enough. He had that brick surrounded. It didn't appear to be going anywhere.

Weenie-dog continued his tirade for about half an hour until we called him to come inside. He then picked the brick up (his lower jaw fit exactly into the brick hole) and brought it in, pleased to death with himself.

I threw it out.

Every time he went out after that he tried to bring the brick in, which is actually quite an effort because coming up the step when you're that short is a real chore even when you're not carrying a pound of rock.

When he's in the yard he picks the brick up and carries it around. Occasionally he flings it and then chases it down and barks at it for a while.

I feel like the brick is a member of the family.

The turtles, on the other hand, mind their own business and do not chase anything but the earthworms I give them as a treat.

It occurred to me recently that the dog might think the brick is a turtle and he's just being patient until the turtle comes out to play.

Companion pup or hound from Hades?

This is what I thought would happen.

I'd get a puppy companion for our 11-year-old weenie-dog Sam. They would stroll through the back yard together.

They would curl up together for long naps on the floor in front of the French doors where the sunshine in during the afternoon. At night they would snuggle in the quilt on the floor of our bedroom.

They would be happy.

The puppy would breathe a little joie de vivre into Sam's otherwise boring life.

After an exhaustive search of local shelters, rescuers, roadsides and friends, I discovered there was a troubling shortage of Lowcountry female wieners.

After more searching that I would ever have believed

necessary, I was forced to drive to the distant village of Rock Hill to get our new canine baby, an eight-week old described to us by her owners as having "a cute personality."

She's cute all right.

We think of her as "the foreigner."

She's from "off." More correctly, she is "off."

Instead of strolling through the back yard with Sam, she rides through the back yard ON Sam.

As he walks by, Sally takes a yapping leap onto his back. He becomes a bucking bronco as she digs in with needlelike toenails and hangs on for dear life. He throws her off and runs as fast as he can to hide behind either me or the Hubster.

Instead of curling up together in the quilt at night, the foreigner pounces on Sam's head, motivating him to sleep on the couch in the den out of leaping range.

The people from whom we acquired the foreigner called her Rachel.

She's not a "Rachel."

We soon realized that "a cute personality" in Rock Hill, due to cultural differences between the northern and coastal parts of the state, means something different here. She is now called a host of things, none of which is Rachel.

For a solid week the Hubster and I had conversations

consisting of eight words or less.

"What about Delilah?" he'd ask.

My response: "No."

We examined lists in baby name books. We racked our brains and each other's nerves.

"What about Madison? What about Tulip?"

As we fell asleep I muttered things like "What about Xena? Xena would be good."

"Never," was the reply from under the pillow next to me.

"Allie…like alley cat?"

"Go to sleep," was the groaning response.

Yesterday we were in the middle of a conversation about Manchild #2's impending SAT exams.

"What's the next test date?" the Hubster asked.

"Sally?" I responded.

The Hubster decided he'd had enough and said,

"OK. Sally it is."

"But do you like that or are you just saying you like it because you're tired of talking about it?" I whined.

"Doesn't matter. Her name is Sally." He picked her up and said, "Want some lunch, Sally?"

He has made it plain that unless someone comes up with an overwhelmingly better name, the puppy will hitherto be known as Sally. I can't help but wonder what Sam would call her if he could talk.

Like mother, like weenie dog

The assignment: Gather up as many members of the household as possible and take them to have their auras read. To tell you the truth, I didn't know I had an aura and I sure didn't think the Hubster or any of our men-children had anything as dainty as an aura.

Aroma? Sure, but not an aura.

I approached my beloved.

"Sweetie, how about giving up a couple of hours on the boat renovation Saturday," I asked.

"What for," he asked suspiciously.

"You can go with me to have your aura read," I explained.

His response: "Not gonna' happen."

It was as simple as that.

Next, I hit on our 20-something child, Surfer Dude and got

his usual response: "Gotta surf."

Our youngest, Man-Child No. 2, explained to me in the condescending tone that only a teen-ager can muster, "Mommmm, guys don't have auras."

About then our herd of weenie dogs came barreling through the kitchen.

Sam-the-Senior weenie is gender-challenged when it comes to auras, so I ruled him out.

Mable, our matronly roadside find, didn't seem interested. (She probably figures her many months living off the fat of the land and roadside litter are the only new experiences she needs for a while.)

Then there was one-year-old, Sally, the weenie princess, turning mid-air flips to attract my attention and finally resorting to riding weenie-Sam bareback. (Sally really needs a miniature cowgirl hat and little cowgirl boots with spurs. YEE-HAH.) She was practically screaming "Me! Me! I need my aura read!

It was pretty obvious Sally was up for the adventure.

Saturday morning on the day of the reading, Sally and I had a chat as I brushed her long hair. I explained she needed to find her inner serene place so she wouldn't have a bad reading. She barked sincerely into my face and licked my nose

(I hate that.)

We chose ensembles of hot pink for the occasion: my blouse and her leash-and-collar duo.

Once on the road, instead of taking the usual interstate, we took the moss-draped oak and preserved plantations road.

"We'll take the scenic highway, so we will be relaxed and get our auras right," I told Sally. Our destination was a small shop at which an aura reader would find out all about us by reading our auras from a special Polaroid photo.

I know I was excited and you could just see the enthusiasm in Sally's face. But then Sally is enthusiastic about the wind, squirrels, watching the grass grow – she's a very passionate animal.

Sally greeted the photo-aura-psychic by wagging her tail so hard her whole body was in frantic motion.

I opted for just a handshake instead.

Sally was first up. Aura-guy placed her on the chair atop a card table that made her the right height (Sally is approximately 10 inches tall at her apex) for the reader's pre-positioned camera. I told Sally to stay – and she did. I was dumbstruck. (Apparently our morning chat worked.) He took the photo.

Next up, me. I smiled, he clicked.

Once our photos had time to develop, psychic-guy carefully explained the lovely colors splotched all over our photographs. Mine glowed with a lovely shade of turquoise, which pleased me since turquoise is very fashionable this season.

The blue, he explained, indicated self-expression (I could go with that – and it didn't seem like a particularly huge deduction to figure that out since I write for a living).

The gold that hovered at the bottom of my photo meant I was an evolved being (I've been telling the Hubster that for years.). The orange indicated creativity (That was a relief.)

Mr. Psychic then turned to Sally.

Her photo featured a red area around her head. Jones frowned a little then said, "Sally seems to have a lot of youthful energy. And the orange shows a passionate and adventurous personality."

"No joke," I responded. Sally licked my chin and tried to leap to the floor by way of my back.

"And she has the same spiritual aura that you have. Pets usually have the same spiritual aura as their owners," he concluded.

So what I found out from the reading is that I am a creative person with an evolved spirit that is apparently identical to the evolved spirit that belongs to my one-year-old weenie dog.

That's just great.

Dog with two heads

There was a time when a lizard came every afternoon between 1 and 2:30 to sit on the kitchen wall phone next to our sliding glass patio door. (I finally decided he was a soap opera fan that was partial to "Days of Our Lives" which was my secret passion.)

This particular day, the lizard was sitting there minding his own business when the phone rang. The ringing gave the lizard a start, and he disappeared. I picked up the phone to say hello to my friend Gail.

About then Our Dog Sam – a wee weenie dog about the size of a roll of Jimmy Dean sausage – started screaming at the top of his lungs and turning in circles in the floor in front of me like a Ferris Wheel with Chucky at the controls.

"Gotto go," I told Gail and slammed down the phone.

The kids (10 and 6 years old at the time) ran in to see what was up. We three stood there in rapt amazement as the dog continued to whirl and making this crazy yodeling screeching sound.

"What's wrong with Sam?" the oldest shouted over the din. The three of us raced around the room trying to catch and calm the dog but he was too quick and obviously out of his mind.

"Calm down, Sam, quiet down." We tried to reach for him and he turned further away in abject terror.

We all pleaded with him as we tried to catch him to comfort and calm him down.

"What's wrong, Sam, what's wrong?

(I wonder what we'd have done if Sam had turned around and answered us?)

About then I saw something dangling from Sam's head.

"He has something stuck to his face," Manchild #2 observed.

I leaned down closer to the floor to get a look at what was on his face as Sam continued to go berserk.

Well, there was a lizard attached to the soft jowls of our puppy's face. The lizard had a bite-hold, his thin reptile tail flying in the wind as Sam revolved around and around.

The kids by then were crying and wailing for me to intervene and to do something that indicated someone was in charge.

"Get him off his face, Mommy. Get the lizard off Sam!" by then they were beginning to grab at me, at each other in a panic.

Amid dog screeching and children blubbering, I grabbed an afghan from the chair and threw it over Sam's wiener torso, leaving his head still visible.

The lizard contentedly dangled from the Sam's face with its spooked-wild-horse look.

About then I remembered a childhood episode of seeing girls attaching lizards to their ears like earrings – the lizards would harmlessly bite and hang there. The girls removed the lizards from their ears by grabbing them behind the neck causing their little reptile jaws (the lizard's, not the girls) to unlock.

I realized I was going to have to touch the lizard (yuk) but weighed against the hysterical dog and distraught children, grabbing the lizard was looking like a pretty good choice. I bent closer to Sam who shied away, but stayed relatively still as I carefully and reluctantly squeezed the lizard's neck between my thumb and index finger. The lizard opened its mouth and I removed it from Sam's face and took it outside to the nearest camellia bush and wished it on its merry way.

Sam, by then, had slipped from the afghan and was hiding under my desk. He refused to come out until the next afternoon. He was probably mulling over how that lizard ended up on his face – my guess is Sam was chasing the lizard, made a grab for it, and the lizard grabbed back.

The lizard did not return to watch his soap opera ever again.

I read in the newspaper's lost and found column a few days later that someone had lost a lizard – a very "large, bearded dragon lizard."

I cast an eye at Sam imagining how much worse his run-in with a lizard could have been.

Do pets keep us awake?

Yes. They do.

How do I know this? Because the health guru on my favorite morning TV show said so – and because we have pets.

Take our weenie dog, Sally, who has made herself right at home in ways that her much beleaguered fellow weenie, Sam, never has – at least until recently.

Sam never slept on our bed. It wasn't allowed. Besides, his 5-inch-long legs never let him jump that high. He has a quilt in the corner of our bedroom.

Then we got Sally. We gave her a blanket in an opposite corner from Sam. But she was insulted. She wanted to sleep with Sam ... or us. Since Sam hid under furniture every time she approached, she chose to bed-partner with us. She scratched and clawed her way to the top of our bed, sat first on my head, then the Hubster's.

After two nights of trying to get her to sleep on the floor, we took the experts' advice and resorted to THE CRATE.

Had we been ripping her legs slowly off of her body she would not have screamed louder. Nothing would soothe her. No ticking clock to simulate the heartbeat of her mother (who resided a five-hour drive away) could quiet her screams. At 3 a.m. on day four of our new-puppy-saga, the Hubster rose from our bed and said: "That's it. I have had enough. I have to get some sleep!"

He took Sally and the crate and disappeared. Ten minutes later he crawled back into the bed. There was no Sally.

"Where is she? What'd you do with her?" I asked, actually fearful for her wellbeing.

"She's in the garage. I put pillows and a quilt on top of the crate to cut down on the noise," he said.

It was quiet, but did we sleep? No. We did not sleep. We lay there in wide-awake silence, side-by-side, flat on our backs, staring at the ceiling, thinking of our poor baby dog in the garage.

In the dark.

In a cage.

In my mind she was still screaming next to the bed.

The next night her howls were twice as bad, penetrating the quilts, pillows and garage door through the length of the house to our room. At 2 a.m. I, too, had had enough and went to the garage and retrieved my animal and planted her on the foot of our bed.

The Hubster looked at me with an accusatory scowl.

"Do not ask. Do not say a word. We are all going to sleep now," I told him.

And we did. She slept like a little princess in her royal bed – all three pounds of her.

Unfortunately, Sam thought this unjust and took to banging his body against the bed until we let him up, also.

So now the four of us are piled up in the bed. Do we get enough sleep? No. Sometimes Sam chases squirrels in his sleep and sometimes Sally still wants to sit on our heads.

So when I saw the good TV doctor, sitting in bed with his dog Scooter, recently, he had my attention right away.

I sat on the edge of our own dog-strewn bed (Sam and Sally were having a sleep-in that morning, while the Hubster and I made plans to go to work) and listened to this astute man discuss why Americans don't get enough sleep. It seems we don't get enough sleep not because of the TV or too much caffeine or rich food or undisciplined nighttime hours. We can't sleep because our pets sleep with us.

A sleep expert and the expert's dog Mozart then joined the doctor on the set. This doctor reported a study indicating that 75 percent of people who have pets, sleep with them, and that is the reason Americans don't get enough sleep. The animals are up and down all night, eating and drinking and making merry (or chasing dream squirrels).

I kept waiting for them to offer a solution to the problem, but what they concluded was: It's fine to sleep with your pet.

"You can't really reap the health benefits of having a pet if you don't spend time with it."

I looked at our two, lolling on their backs, legs spread to the wind, smirky smiles on their faces.

I think what we have here is a classic case of the tail wagging the people.

Unromantic night with crazed dogs

The night was made for romance. There we were. We'd been in bed just a little while when the storm started. Lightning flashed (lots of lightning) and thunder turned the heavens into the underside of a bowling alley.

Rain pounded above like cat-eye marbles being dumped on the roof.

Romantic. Yes, it was.

Except for three things – our herd of wieners. They didn't think it was all that romantic. Sam the senior weenie had no notion that anything was even going on since he's blind and deaf. He snoozed happily at the foot of the bed.

Sally the Princess Weenie just figured the racket was her invitation to frolic and commenced running back and forth up and down the length of the bed, stopping at each end, ears thrown back, eyes wild with excitement then reversing the romp.

Mabel didn't find the racket amusing, interesting, boring or anything else. Mabel, who usually sleeps on the opposite end of the house from us, awakened by the mayhem, she left her nest and arrived in our room. We could hear her padding around the bed, looking for a way up. Since she can't make the leap on her own and realizing her panic, I picked her up and placed her at the foot of the bed with the others.

She crept immediately up my leg. I put her back at the foot of the bed and reminded her to stay, which under usual circumstances, she would do.

Then the thunder boomed again and up she came. There she was whining and panting and looking deranged and creeping back up to the head of the bed. She was hyperventilating. I turned the lights on to see what she was doing and where all the canine parties were located. The thunder roared again and Mabel's panic burst into full bloom.

Instead of creeping, she now galloped to the head of the bed.

I decided to embrace the situation, instead of The Hubster. I gathered Mabel into my arms and hugged her tight. But that wouldn't do. Apparently the only place Mabel felt safe was sitting on my head, which, quite frankly, I wasn't up for no matter how desperate she was. So I moved her back down. The storm railed on. I'd finally had enough and put her back on the floor, at which time she started hurling herself at the bed and barking.

The situation was definitely deteriorating.

Sally took the barking and jumping about to mean that Mabel would like to play with her, so Sally leaped off the bed and landed all fours astraddle Mabel's back. It was playtime. Mabel, mistaking Sally's landing on her as meaning that whatever was creating all that heavenly racket was now actually launching an attack on her. She let out a howling yelp and a snarly sound. Sally started barking along with Mabel's yelps. By then, even Sam was awake. The doggy bedlam joined with the crashing of thunder, the pounding of rain and the howls of The Hubster who suddenly sprang to life. (Had he actually fallen asleep in the middle of all this?)

"I'm going to go sleep on the couch," he mumbled. I grabbed his arm and said, "Think again."

He wasn't leaving me in there with dogs gone wild.

And then it happened. The storm stopped. Demented wieners turned docile. They happily snuggled at the foot of the bed. I sat there, lamp on, arms crossed and watched in amazement as all four wieners (three dogs and a guy) began snoring.

Romantic?

Right.

What dogs, husbands, dream of

The paperback book at the grocery store had been teasing me for weeks. There it was, with the cute little border collie on the front, smiling up at me under the titles, "What Do Dogs Dream About?"

"I will not buy that book," I said out loud to myself the first week I saw it.

The next week, surprised the book was still in the rack, I repeated the same mantra. I made a halfhearted mental note that is if the book was not gone the following week, I would buy it.

The third week, the man in front of me took forever to sort out his coupons, write a check, then chat up the cashier.

There the smiling dog sat. I tried not to look. Finally, I picked it up and said, "come on puppy, you're going on home with me."

So I've been eagerly reading the book trying to find out what's going on in the minds of our weenies as they yip, flail and chase down dream squirrels in their sleep.

The book quotes a doctor as saying dogs just review what has happened during the day, although their dreams probably don't help them resolve issues like human dreams sometimes do.

What I found more interesting than the dream part (which was actually pretty thin and boring) was the part titled, "If only they had listened."

It's about owners who should have listened to their dogs.

Our dachshunds tried to alert us to a situation that was developing over the last few weeks, but we didn't listen because we don't speak dog. If they'd been speaking English, or maybe even German, then we'd have listened. (We also would have gotten them an agent.)

Several weeks ago, Sally the Princess Weenie and her cohort Mabel took to racing out the back door and barking at the back of the house. I finally went out and looked. I saw nothing but the covered gas grill. They appeared to be barking at a blank brick wall.

Maybe they were barking at the scent of barbecues past.

That theory worked just fine until the Hubster went outside to get the grill fired up to cook our dinner. He opened the grill cover, brushed off the rack with a steel brush and was greeted by a tiny little field mouse that poked its head up through the grill, then beat a hasty retreat to the unlighted lava rocks below.

"It 'bout scared me to death. I nearly dropped my tenderloin," the Hubster said. "But it (the mouse, not the tenderloin) jumped to the back row of unlighted rocks.

"Then I turned that row on, too, and the mouse jumped out of the grill and scooted into the woodpile," my live-in cook said, indicating our disorderly stack of deadfall piled against the fence.

Now the dogs spend a majority of their outdoor time in the woodpile after first running out the back door and barking heartily at the grill.

If we'd listened to our dogs, who obviously were trying to alert us to the homeless mouse that had set up housekeeping in the grill, the Hubster wouldn't have been startled half to death.

And maybe he wouldn't have been so restless the last few nights – even calling out in his sleep – which is all pretty darned unusual because it's his nature to sleep soundly anytime, anywhere.

What I could use now is a book titled "What do husbands dream about?"

Probably a bed that isn't littered with disturbed hot dogs and grills that haven't been turned into condos.

Pet peeves driving us crazy

As it turns out, wiener dogs get freaked out about stuff, but not the same stuff.

For instance, Charlotte is not a big fan of the Hubster's harmonica.

"Everyone's a critic," he said the other day as Charlotte ran in circles growling in response to whatever tune it was her master was playing.

She was not dancing.

She was looking for a place to hide.

I got the impression that had she been able, she would have leaped up and snatched the blues harp from his mouth and buried it in her mole hole excavation site in the back yard. But when you're only 10 inches tall at your high point, that isn't a real option.

Sally, on the other hand, responds in a big way to noises. If she hears a dog barking on TV, she's convinced it's in the room with her, pricks up her ears and starts barking back. She has the same routine for TV doorbells with the added extra of hopping down from the couch and running to the front door where she turns in circles and basically goes insane.

Sam-the-Senior-Weenie, on the other hand, starts shivering and trembling and looking for a place to hide, going around-and-around on his blanket until he finds just the right spot under which to dive.

If the elements or electronics aren't getting our dogs riled up, then the Hubster takes up the slack. It is, in fact, his mission to find out what entertains the dogs (in addition to the harmonica) and then do it until it makes them (and me) crazy.

Like the other night when he whipped out the red laser pointer he uses for targeting things like pie charts and people who burp in public.

He shined the tiny bright red beam on the floor and wiggled it around to get Charlotte's attention. She leaped on it like a cat. He had her chasing it all over the room. (I was ready to chase both of them right out of the house or do something with the red laser pointer that the Hubster would likely have found it offensive.)

Then Sally noticed it and figured something was trying to hurt her baby dog companion and tried to keep Charlotte from getting close to the red dot. Sally looked like she was herding sheep as she stayed close to Charlotte.

They went round-and-round in circles.

I mentioned that in addition to driving the dogs nuts, he also was making me crazy, so he put pointer away, whipped out his harmonica and started playing a tune.

I joined the dogs as we all went in circles.

I think I have discovered the origins of dancing.

Welcoming new dog in the family

I've discovered the missing link. It started when I picked up a lost dog on the side of the road, a rural road, on a solo visit to my parents at their lake cabin.

Concerned for her safety as pickup trucks and boat-toting jeeps passed, I pulled off the narrow road and slowly made my way over to her, not wanting to scare her away. She timidly came to me and gently I bundled her into my car. I went up and down the sparsely populated roads, going house-to-house as I made repeated unsuccessful attempts to find the owner of this sweet, withdrawn bag-of-bones.

She wore a very old, heavy leather collar that dangled loosely from her neck. It was obviously meant for a much larger dog than she…or she had lost an unbelievable amount of weight. Probably both.

No one knew whose dog she was. I went to a nearby campground.

We stopped by my sister's house who lived several miles down the road. I knew she and her husband, animal lovers to a fault, would have dog food and maybe some suggestions of who the owner could be. They had the food, but nothing more.

We spent the next few days at the river cabin. She ate only a little but seemed to gain strength. I posted fliers but when it came time to go back home, I was resigned to take her home with me. It looked like we would have a new addition to our wiener entourage. It could be an interesting arrival back home.

Home again, home again

The long road home to the Hubster and our men-in-training was filled with questions.

- Would the Hubster pitch a tent in the back yard and put the dog and me in it to live together?
- Could I sneak the new addition in?
- Would she blend in with the other two weenie dogs and no one would notice? (Boy, do I live in a fantasy world.)

Once home, I took a deep breath, opened the front door (I left New-Dog in the car for the time being) and checked out my family's whereabouts. Naturally, the whole pile of them, who are usually not to be found anywhere, were sitting in the den, waiting for me like I was bringing home dinner. My hopes of sneaking the dog in waned.

"You're acting funny. What's wrong?" my guy asked.

"I brought you a surprise," I told my beloved.

"What kind of surprise?" he asked skeptically. It's not alive, is it?"

"Well, uh, actually, it is." I went out to the car and brought in the black-and-tan dachshund that I'd been nursing back to health over the weekend. He looked her over, petted her and said, "I was afraid it might be a cat," the Hubster said, referring to my love of, and allergy to, cats. "What're you gonna' do with her," he asked.

"Keep her until I find her folks?" I half-stated, half-asked.

"And her folks are where?" the Hubster asked.

"Don't know. Might not find them. Might have to keep her."

About then Sally jumped on New-Dog's back, and the newcomer let her know that such behavior was highly inappropriate. Sam the ancient weenie sniffed and walked off. Big deal.

By Tuesday, Man-Child Number 2 had named New-Dog, Marquesas "the Survivor." It didn't stick 'cause she just wasn't that exotic – a little more down to earth than that. So we settled on Mabel. A good solid name.

Mabel has seen hard times and knows how to fend for herself.

She knows where the bag of dog food is and isn't shy about getting her own breakfast.

Her counterparts watch in horror. They've never had to get their own food. They've never wanted for anything except maybe an extra dollop of gravy. Mabel makes it plain she will eat first.

A low food-related growl is the only noise that came from her for the first five days. No whining or barking (hard times: not much to bark about). No jumping or frolicking. No wagging of tail. (It was obvious that to poor starving Mabel, tail wagging was a luxury.)

Survival was her only motivation.

But a few days in, she wagged her tail and barked, a low-pitched, throaty bark.

My mother called last night. "How's the dog doing? She sure is a quiet little thing," she said. "She probably thinks she died and went to heaven," Momma said.

Well, I never thought of our house as heaven, but I guess it beats drinking ditch water and living in the underbrush in the cold.

Mabel gained weight; she found her place in our home (and the foot of the bed with the others; the Hubster made sounds about upsizing the bed). In one week's time she established herself as a friend to the old dog and a playmate to the baby dog – our missing link.

I hope someone somewhere is missing her. I hate to think she was just thrown away.

She really is a sweet girl.

Sweet Mabel

Soon after I returned home from the cabin with Mabel we headed off to the vet. The vet said he couldn't be sure about her age, but she was at least 9 years old. And she wasn't a well dog. He said we should take her home, see if she could regain some strength, and live out whatever time she had left with us.

She became known as Mabel, a friend to Sam the Senior Wiener and playmate to Sally the Princess Wiener. She blossomed into a loving pet, going from a silent, withdrawn, nearly starved lost soul – or throwaway – to a healthy, bouncy dachshund that loved to dig holes with her stepsister Sally. She seemed happy and was loved.

Mabel departed her life and ours after only a year. She went to sleep and didn't wake up.

Sister Sally didn't understand.

In the days following Mabel's departure, Sally tore around the back yard, barking for her friend to come play, looking for her in the doghouse and at the site of their favorite dig.

After a few minutes Sally would give up, come in and lie on the floor, head on her paws, deep in thought.

Last week when we introduced Sweet Charlotte, the reactions were predictable. Sam, in true guy-dog form, sniffed the air and stayed as far away as possible.

Charlotte presented an irritation to his tranquil life. Charlotte was beneath him. (Literally. She could run under him, and Sam has less than a 6-inch clearance.)

Sally took to Sweet Charlotte immediately, mothering and playing with the two-pound, fearless puppy.

Sally has always seemed to want a puppy to mother, caring for her soft toys and putting them in a basket as if telling them goodnight before bed.

Now Sally has her puppy. She allows Charlotte to chew on her face, nibble on her ears and pull her tail. Sally is the perfect mother, even trying to lift her adopted offspring into the house. She's even tried to teach Sweet Charlotte to dig, but Charlotte is young and would rather jump on Sally's back and play than attend to the serious business of unearthing underground dwellers.

Yesterday, Sally went out to the back yard alone.

She headed to her digging corner and made a halfhearted attempt at digging up whatever it is she and Mabel were always after. After a couple of minutes she walked away to the other corner of the back yard, the corner where her friend was laid to rest.

Sally sniffed around for a few seconds, bewildered, before coming back to the house.

As Sally came in, Charlotte romped over to greet her before trying to climb on her back.

Sally licked the puppy's face and raced back out the door. Charlotte followed as fast as her 2-inch-long legs would take her.

Sally began to dig again and, for the first time, Charlotte tried to help.

Training puppy all in timing

The column today should be consumed ONLY as a between-meal snack. It should NOT, under any circumstance, be taken with breakfast, lunch or dinner. Today, we are discussing the unifying factor of all living things; something that became a part of our lives immediately after our first child was born. Our first clue to what would be our new favorite topic of conversation came when the baby nurse came into my hospital room in the military hospital in Landstuhl, Germany, and asked if the baby had, well, you know ... pooped.

Our lives from that moment forward revolved around the intake and output of our much-doted-on baby and the containment and disposal thereof (not of the baby, but of the remains of our child's diet).

There was much agonizing over, and experimentation

with, the types of disposable diapers that would most efficiently keep our precious baby comfy. (This earnest interest in his output was a source of discussion between us for several years until his brother came along and made us realize there was more than one baby pooping in the world.)

Of course, we are way past the baby stage now, but lest we be at a loss for something to do, we went out and got Sweet Charlotte, a longhaired red dachshund puppy. Charlotte weighs about 2 pounds, most of which, apparently, is on the move, so to speak. So to love Charlotte is to love – poop.

The workings of Charlotte's innards are almost as important to us as the innards of our first guy-child's once upon a time were. Our most important task at this point is to be sure Charlotte does not bestow any presents for us on the floor, but learns instead to make her deposits in a special area of the back yard.

Let me just say this, timing is everything.

Our entire lives now revolve around monitoring and discussing Charlotte's outflow. For instance, Sunday night, it was cold and the wind was blowing.

"How long has it been since she went out?" the Hubster asked.

After way more discussion than was appropriate, we decided it had been half an hour. In the midst of our debate, we lost track of Charlotte's whereabouts, which is pretty easy since she's so tiny and matches the wood floor.

"It's your turn," I said, pulling my sweater more tightly around me and hoping my guy would go for that.

"I took her out last time," he reminded me.

I finally grabbed a coat, slipped into shoes and called the puppy. She came running, an innocent look on her upturned face. I tucked her under my arm since she is too short to exit the house on her own without taking a header onto the concrete – a steep drop of eight inches.

Although a patio lamp lights the backyard, it is not enough illumination to see the infant dog's miniature presents. So I carried a mega-lumen flashlight with which to observe. I knew when I went back into the house I would be questioned and would have to give a detailed description to my partner-in-house-training.

On this occasion Charlotte's gift was nearly invisible. I praised her lavishly for being so efficient and quick.

I returned to the house. The Hubster was scrubbing the floor. He did not ask for a description.

Timing truly is everything.

Little wieners and other tails

Sally and Charlotte have one goal in life: To be sure I'm never without something to do. It's their lot in life and they take it seriously.

Really.

If I sit in my comfy chair to read, watch TV or write, Sally immediately wants to join me, so I pick her up and put her beside me and get comfy again. About time I'm settled and Sally has stopped wandering around in her half of the chair as she tries to get just right, Charlotte trots in to notice her sister is getting more attention that she is. So I put down the book or the computer or remote and lift her up to the chair and line her up next to Sally.

Then I wait for them both to stop milling around in their half of the chair. Eventually they end up right where they started and I go back to doing whatever I was doing.

But then a squirrel scampers across the patio or a bird alights on a bush near the door or the backyard neighbor dog runs the fence and barks to them to come out and play. They bolt out of the chair like crazy dogs and have a flying duck fit to go outside.

I put down the book, etc. and go to the door to let them out. They streak out across the backyard in pursuit of whatever has gotten their attention. I return to my chair.

Two minutes later they are at the door. Sally uses the barking method to ask to come in while Charlotte prefers the scratching at the patio window technique. The combination is very effective so I get up again and let them back in. I return to my chair.

They do not immediately return with me. They need a drink of water and a bite of kibble.

A snack.

That takes about a minute, just long enough for me to settle back to my own pursuits.

Then and only then do they come and stand up with their paws on the edge of the chair seat and beg to be lifted back next to me. I lift them one at a time (this is the disadvantage of having dogs with very short legs) and they quickly settle down for a little nap.

I might get to relax ten or so minutes before some other life event intervenes like the neighbors slamming a car door across the street at which time they both leap from the chair and run to the front door to greet guests who will not materialize because they are not our guests but those of our neighbors, a nuance they (our dogs, not our neighbors) have not picked up on yet.

Once again they return to be lifted.

I solved the lifting of the dog onto the sofa situation with the little steps advertised from time-to-time on TV. It took Sally two months to get used to them and now she uses the step only with great reluctance and only after first asking in her-paws-on-the-edge-of-the-seat way to be lifted up.

So I was in the pet store yesterday and found something I'd been looking for: a pet door that slips into place in the sliding glass doors. A panel with a doggy door at the bottom of it. That would solve at least one of the problems.

The Hubster spent the opening hours of his Father's Day installing the door. I spent the remainder of the day trying to coax either of the dogs to actually enter or exit through the portal.

They don't like it and refuse to use it unless I get up and

hold the flap open for them, which, as far as I can figure, negates the reason for having it at all.

So you can imagine my surprise when I came home from work last week to discover the wieners in the house. Now the last person to leave was the Hubster and there's no way he would have left them in.

So I had to assume one thing and one thing only. The wieners had come in through:

• The bathroom window.

• The doggy door I purchased a couple of weeks ago.

Since they're too short to jump through a window, I decided they had come in the way they were supposed to.

"Why would I think otherwise?" you might ask.

Because the week since the purchase of this particular doggy door has not been what I would call a raging success.

Day one, the Hubster installs the door over the course of several hours. It was way more complicated than had been implied by the "just slide into place" message on the box. The process involved screwdrivers and drills and two people. While he screwed and drilled, I built doggy steps on the outside of the doggy door so they wouldn't have so far to step (or fall).

But once it was finished, I placed Sally in front of the door and its little swing flap opening.

She did not go through.

I gave her a nudge. Still she did not go through.

While I nudged Sally, Charlotte alternately watched, ran in a circle and watched again. When I finally pushed Sally through the door into the great outdoors, Charlotte ran and hid in the bedroom under the quilt. She's a little ditzy but as it turns out, she's not particularly stupid.

I went and got Charlotte and repeated the exercise with her, gently pushing her through the door.

They both stared at me from outside then ran to the patio door to be let in. I went outside and pushed them one at a time back into the house through the doggy door.

Off and on during the day we practiced this new trick. (I tried to remember how long it had taken Charlotte to learn to use the doggy steps to get up onto the ottoman. A day maybe?)

The next day after work when the Hubster came home he worked with them a bit on their new equipment.

We finally decided they thought we were playing a game with them and didn't recognize the potential for their own freedom with this new toy.

Eventually they got where they'd go through the flap if

we picked them up and placed them in front of it. That's when we realized they only wanted to "play" the new game if we were playing with them.

That was until Friday when I found them in the house.

Later that night I heard the doggy-door-flap swing and realized one of them had gone outside without being coaxed. A few seconds later, I heard it swing again and knew the other had followed.

Last night as we watched a little Saturday night TV (which, by the way, is nowhere near what it used to be) Charlotte trotted over to the couch and begged the Hubster to put her up there with him.

"Go to the steps," he reminded her.

Charlotte persisted.

That's when the Hubster muttered,

"Charlotte only has room in her tiny little head for one trick at a time and has forgotten how to climb the doggy steps."

I had to agree with him.

Charlotte's a one trick dog.

Put a real flycatcher on the job

Here we sit, my coworkers and I. We are working, or trying to.

Our desks are on the second floor of a huge, mostly windowless building that takes up a city block. We have the same problems as most people in a closed office environment: too cold inside when it's hot outside (and vice versa), stale air and glaring fluorescent lights.

We have no idea whether rain is falling or sun is shining unless we get up and walk over to peer through the small cloudy window in the center back of the acre-size room.

But this week something new flew into the mix.

Monday as I sat at my desk, something bit me on the leg. It was a fly.

"There's a fly in here," I stated to the tops of the heads of my coworkers.

"There's one over here, too, I heard someone mumble from a couple of rows away, an errant hand flailing the air.

How does a fly get to the second floor of a building this size that has front doors, security doors and a mostly elevator mode of ascending and descending?

By Wednesday the fly population had grown and we were swatting the air and complaining. (We love to complain. It's what we do best.)

Friday as I walked toward my desk from the elevator, I was assaulted by a scent. A parmesan-cheese-gone-amok odor.

"Yuck," I said to myself as I got to my chair and logged onto the computer. "What's that putrid smell?"

Several hands flew up from behind computer screens to point at a red-and-yellow piece of paper dangling from the ceiling grid.

"What is it?" I asked.

"Flypaper," was the choral response.

Flypaper? I haven't seen flypaper since I used to visit my grandmother's country store in Stoneboro (near the booming S.C. burgs of Heath Springs, Lancaster and Liberty Hill.) I remember going to Lancaster with my grandmother to see the movie "Gypsy." I think my mother was a little put out that her mother thought the story of a stripper was appropriate entertainment for a 13-year-old. I, on the other hand, thought it was terrific. Grandmomma was cool.

Anyway, her country store had flypaper hung in the corner over the wooden crates filled with glass returnable RC Cola and Orange Crush bottles. The flypaper was a tacky (in both senses of the word) piece of yellow paper that attracted and captured flies.

At our house, where flies have also been out of control this summer, the most athletic of our wiener dogs, the lovely Princess Sally, has taken to snapping flies out of the air.

Her lizard-like technique seems to be about 90 percent effective. Her new pastime does, however, cut down on any possibility that I will ever let her lick me in the face.

At work, the office flypaper that's hanging about 12 feet from my desk, has a trendy red covering with a polka dot grid pattern to expose the yellow paper beneath. There are no flies on the office flypaper.

As I write this there is a fly sitting on my desk watching me write. I anticipate that at any minute it will start offering suggestions about word usage.

I would gladly trade in the stinky, sticky flypaper for a real flycatcher – Sally.

She is effective, cuter, and works for food, lodging, and a kiss – only an air kiss – when she's on the job.

Groomer goes from fluff to fur

Hurricane-inspired rain had been the norm for at least five days, and Princess Sally the wiener dog was way overdue for a backyard digging session. On her final outing that evening, having held off as long as she could, she was overcome with the desire to get down and dirty. Dirty was the operative word. As a result, there I was at 11 p.m., with a dog, plopped knee deep in 2 inches of kitchen sink water, mud leaching out of her fur.

I ran my fingers through her long locks to pull the twigs and leaves from her coat. It seems she had chosen as her dig site the pile of trash left over from the hurricane that missed us three hurricanes back.

Yippee.

I got the bathing job because I am officially in charge of

hair and grooming at our house. I won that position by default. I live in an all-guy household and quite frankly, the state of my guys' hair was always way down on their list of things to worry about, so the chore of worrying about hair was left to me. When the guy-children were little, back in the big-hair-'80s, I had a tendency to blow-dry their hair to a fluffy state. It didn't seem all that big at the time, but looking back on it, the only things bigger than their heads of hair were my shoulder pads. Just recently as we sifted through stacks of old photos, our oldest nearly gagged at the sight of his big blond hairdo, so lovingly blown dry by his overzealous mother. Me. His blond hair eventually turned dark brown. He now wears it as short as he can get it without shaving it. In retrospect, it's easy to see why. His brother, Man-Child No. 2, is still experimenting. Last week, he came in with red streaks in his now-black hair. This week the red was transformed to blond. His styles range anywhere from political candidate to drummer in a rock band.

All that hair angst brought me back to my choice of animals. I wished for hair to coif in addition to my own. I decided I would get elegant long hair female weenies. I would care for the hair of the dogs. It'd be great. Enter Princess Sally.

At first it was fun. Her hair was longish but still easy to

care for.

We are now on year three of the Sally saga. No one told me that her fur would get longer and thicker with each passing year. If I could patent her fur and sell it as a dust mop, I'd make a fortune. (Have you seen those Swiffer things they advertise on TV, the ones that pick up everything from cat hair to Cheetos? Well, we don't need one 'cause we have Sally.

Any given night I can brush her and retrieve pine straw, crushed leaves, foot-long lengths of briar vines and an assortment of refuse she has taken on board during her peregrinations in the back yard. If the hair situation continues to escalate, I expect to pull another whole dog out of her fur before long.

So, as I brush and comb and smooth with an assortment of grooming utensils (she has as many as I do), I keep a watchful eye on her one-year-old adopted little sister Charlotte. (Does Charlotte's hair seem a little longer this week than it did last week?)

This is a reminder to be careful what you wish for, because you know what? You just might get it.

Now where's that undercoat brush?

And whose crazy dog is this?

This past weekend we went to Camden for a bridal shower for the daughter of my Best Friend Forever Mary Ann.

Part of the weekend included some time at the lake. I was in charge of getting myself and the wiener dogs to the event while The Hubster arrived on the pontoon boat from its home dock. (Unlike the sailboat, this boat actually runs, and is available for people to ride and have fun on. It requires no maintenance to speak of other than a quick hosing down at the beginning of the season. It is not pretty or elegant. It just works.)

Anyway, while the Hubster was frolicking on the boat, I was getting the wild weenies out of their travel kennel at the party house when Sally decided to take off. I tried to catch her but she raced around the house. On the porch, one of the guests whom I had never actually met, saw us go past.

"Chasing the dog," I called to him as I passed. He waved, apparently not knowing what to make of the situation.

Inside, guests were visiting and having a nice glass of sweet ice tea.

Outside, Sally rounded the house and took off running down the middle of the dirt road with me in hot pursuit. And I do mean hot. It must have been 100 degrees out there. I was dressed for a party, not a sprint, in my red strappy sandals, white pants and shirt.

Sally headed into the woods at the edge of the lake. I couldn't get to her because there was a newly scraped red-mud ditch right in front of me, and beyond that a brush-pile of dried branches and weeds.

Now, Sally has always been a sprinter. I've chased her around our neighborhood more times than I can remember. But last year she had back surgery, didn't walk for months, but eventually recovered 90 percent.

Sally also used to swim like a fiend, she loved it, would run off the end of the dock and leap into the water, ears flapping in the breeze – but that, too, is a thing of the past since her hind legs don't work that well. So swimming for her means we have to give her hind-side a boost so she has the illusion of swimming on her own.

Only problem with that is, she doesn't know she can't swim.

So when I watched her disappear into a brush pile at the water's edge, I panicked. Then I heard her splash into the water. My heart sank and my body went into action. Determined to save my weenie, I leaped across the muddy ditch, missed the mark and came down somehow on both my bottom, my left knee, right hand and left ankle. It was easy to see where I hit since each point of impact was clearly marked on my white garb in bright red mud. Lovely.

When I fell, Sally ran toward me. Then I looked up at her, she saw I was okay and took off again.

I pulled myself to my feet and chased on. Four doors down she ran out of steam and reluctantly came to me.

I clicked the leash to her collar and started the trek home, mumbling the whole way, "How dare you not come when I call you. You could have been killed. What do you think you were doing? You can't swim you crazy animal…." and on and on for the super-sweaty walk home.

Back at the house the partygoers were horrified when I walked in looking like the losing end of a mud-wrestling tournament.

A couple of guests said they'd seen me run by outside, but

thought I was just getting a little exercise.

They had no idea about the drama taking place , they said.

They felt terrible.

About then, the Hubster came cruising up to the dock on the pontoon boat, waving happily and greeting everyone with a wave of his straw hat.

He tied up and came walking toward me, noticed that something was amiss and was about to ask when I shoved the leash into his hand.

"Here's your favorite dog!"

Wild wieners' evening dance

We love our wild wieners.

Most of the time. (Well, all of the time actually. It's just that sometimes it's harder than others.)

They have distinct personalities.

Charlotte is ditsy and cute with long red hair. She always has this very bemused, expectant look on her pretty little face. She's very cheerleader-like in her attitude and carriage. Add a couple of pom-poms and she'd be good to go as a Dallas Cheerleader. She cocks her head sideways when you talk to her.

You would be hard-pressed to find a more endearing dog.

Sally, on the other hand, is the brains. She has a tendency to look rather bored with the antics of the other canine – and human-folk – who just happen to live with her. It's her house, after all. Not mine, or ours. Hers.

If she had opposing thumbs, she would rule the world.

She's not afraid of thunder and is not upset by the rain. While Charlotte is very hesitant to get her dainty feet wet, and with a good loud clap of thunder goes nuts, starts shaking, whimpering and trying to actually crawl up the front of the Hubster or me during a storm, Sally prefers to go out for a walk. She saunters around the backyard as if she's having a stroll in a sunny park on a warm spring day. I swear, if she could laugh out loud, she would.

The biggest challenge is dinnertime.

They each have a bowl. They are expected to eat from that bowl only. (Yeah, right.) And occasionally that happens.

But usually it's a fruit basket turnover situation in which each will eat at their appropriate bowl for a minute or so, then change places, sniff carefully and continue eating. The little dinner dance continues until all the food is gone.

It is obvious to anyone watching that in their minds, they think their sibling dog MUST have something completely more fabulous than what is in their very own dish.

There was a time when we had one big food bowl for our three dogs. When we acquired Charlotte the Wonder Weenie, we went to three small matching bowls for their food. While

Princess Sally ate regular dog food, Charlotte was still on puppy food and Sam ate the Senior Dog formula. (Are dogs so politically aware that they'd be loath to eat something called Food for Old Dogs?)

At first we placed the bowls in a little row of three, deposited the food in each and placed the appropriate dog in front of his or her food. Sam started eating and Charlotte stopped bouncing around long enough to eat. Sally waited for a minute to be sure everyone else was on task, then started on hers.

At that point we left them alone. When we returned to check on them, we discovered they had played a little game and were now eating from each others' bowls.

As we watched, they shifted again so they were eating from different bowls still. While they were perfectly fine with this arrangement, we were not. We put them back at the appropriate eating posts.

Within a couple of days, we acknowledged that feedings weren't going well.

Divide and conquer became our new motto. We left Sam's bowl in its original spot and moved the other two doggie dishes to opposite corners of the kitchen. It worked for a couple of minutes. Then they rambled around the kitchen in their usual feeding rotation.

They were wieners enjoying a buffet of dog foods, grazing from dish to dish. They were guests at a cocktail party sampling hors d'oeuvres. (Had they been toting miniature martini glasses in their little paws, it would not have looked out of place.)

The Hubster and I watched, fascinated. We decided to enforce the rules and herded them back to their own dishes. Finally convinced they were on track, we went into the dining room to have our own dinner. After a few minutes, we checked back.

"Isn't that Sam's bowl," my beloved observed, pointing to bowl No. 1.

"It is," I replied.

"Then why is Sally eating out of it?"

I shrugged my shoulders.

"And this is Charlotte's bowl," I said pointing to the dish from which Sam was chowing down.

Meanwhile, Charlotte crunched away at the food in Sally's dish.

Our new plan is to prepare each bowl, but to put only one on the floor at a time. Sam the Senior Weenie goes first. When he's finished, he goes outside. We then invite Charlotte in for dinner. Once she has finished and left the building, it's Sally's turn.

It is a time-intensive feeding system, but at least it takes place in the kitchen. It could be worse.

My friend Mindy has one dog, Lucy, who refuses to eat in the kitchen. She (the dog, not Mindy) sits at the kitchen door and whines at her dish until Mindy moves it (the dish, not the door) to the dining room. Except for one unexplained night, she will not, under any circumstances enter the kitchen.

"That night, Lucy followed me into the kitchen and ate as if she did so all the time. Everything was fine. I praised her and loved on her, but the next day she went back to sitting at the door and whining at her bowl in the kitchen as if the night before had never happened."

So, it seems whether there is one dog or three, feeding can be a challenge because basically, we don't know what they are thinking. And quite frankly, I'm not sure knowing would help, but at least we'd have a clue.

Wouldn't we?

So the sampling goes on.

Because, they are, after all, wild wieners. Our wild wieners. And we really do love them.

Most of the time.

Adopting, adapting to wiener

I was looking up a tidbit of information on the Internet one day for a story about pet rescues when I came across a picture of Cassie. She looked adorable and very much like Sally our lead wiener. I fell in love, so for a couple of weeks I e-mailed back and forth with the rescue group located in the Rock Hill area. (Yeah, yeah, I know we have plenty of adoptable dogs here, but I was already smitten with this one.)

I filled out the owner survey form so the rescue group could assess whether or not we would be good parents. I was half expecting a home visit from a social worker before it was over, which would have been bad since the Hubster didn't know about our impending new arrival.

But once we were accepted in private, I started cajoling the Hubster right out loud.

"She's so adorable," I told him. "Remember how much

fun it was when we had Mable?" Three dogs had seemed just the right number. It had been at least a year since Mable, our roadside adoptee, had passed away.

I pleaded the Mable angle for a couple more weeks all the while checking to be sure she was still available.

My guy finally said "maybe."

"If Cassie's still there by the end of the month, then we'll go look at her," he said.

So every day, I checked the Website to see if she was there, and she was. At the end of the two weeks, we headed for York County, the birthplace of our new dog.

"Now remember, this is just to look at her," he reminded me.

I was already planning to get new matching food bowls for the three of them, and leashes and figuring out how to walk all three at the same time.

"Sure. Only if we really, really like her," I agreed out loud.

But inside I was thinking about how to manage all three when we went on vacation to the lake.

"If she's not the right fit, we can look at other dogs," he continued.

And I was figuring out if we really had room for all three dogs to sleep at the foot of the bed.

"Cause she's not the only dog out there," the Hubster said.

And I could get a new doggie bed that would fit all three more comfortably.

"We can look around for a while to be sure," he continued.

Yeah, right. That was going to happen.

Once in York County we got lost for about an hour, asked directions three times, but finally found the rescue facilty buried in the woods, a beautiful setting for orphan dogs.

When we first saw Cassie, she looked just like Sally. But it didn't take long to discover the difference. This dog was an athlete, a high jumper, a sprinter. She was mighty quick on her feet and wanted to get some loving in a big way.

And as you might have guessed, we now have three dogs.

Cassie stares at me, eyes half closed, in the most pitiful "please love me" way that obviously works for her since I rub her head in the way she has taught me. It's pretty obvious that someone, somewhere used to rub her head every night after dinner.

She's not exactly like the others.

She can jump about four feet off the ground, most often against the glass patio doors. We figure she's one part dachshund and four parts pogo stick.

She's not exactly what we expected, so, we've had to go out of our way to get to know her, to appreciate the differences inherent in whatever extra breed is part of her makeup. She's learning to adapt to our ways as well.

And she jumps. Boy, can she jump.

Some things better left alone

It seemed like a great idea at the time. The plan was to bring Sam the Weenie Dog in for a photo shoot with me.

Sure. We could do that.

The night before the planned studio shoot, I decided a little hair color touch-up was in order. I went over to my nearby mega-deluxe-grocery store to pick up my usual shade of brown. I stood before the shelves and examined the rainbow of colors from all the different brands. Then, as always, I chose the same one I've been using all along and turned to go check out.

That's when I saw it.

The Just for Men display.

Just brush it on, the instructions said. It promised a five-minute time capsule that would return anyone to the handsome youthfulness of years past.

Sam could use a little touch-up, too, I thought. And he's a guy.

Sam's face had gone almost white with doggy gray. I selected a color that seemed to match his pretty red coat. His face would once again be the color from puppyhood.

I would do the color job the next morning before work.

At 6:10 a.m. swimmer boy had been hustled off to high school (who in the world sets these hours?), and I headed for the dog. Weenie dog was a little surprised to be the object of so much attention before 7 a.m.

I picked him up and sweet-talked him all the way to the bathroom.

He stood on the countertop, uncertainty shading his eyes as I mixed up the color concoction according to instructions.

Then with the little brush provided by the Just for Men folks, I carefully coated his snout and jowls, leaving a no-dye-zone around his big brown eyes, which by then were worriedly gazing at me.

He was a skeptical dog.

Once finished, I wrapped him in a blanket with his snout sticking out and carried him into the den to watch the early news show, which we did huddled together in the chair for five minutes.

We returned to the bathroom.

I unveiled Sam's new look.

It wasn't good.

It really wasn't good.

It was awful.

To say I panicked would be mild. I about died. I wiped his cute weenie face with tissues. I rinsed, I scrubbed. I chattered away at him, apologizing over and over.

He looked like a raccoon. His face was black with wide white circles around his eyes.

About then the Hubster walked into the bathroom, having just awakened.

"Whatcha' doin'?" he asked, still half asleep.

"I did something bad," I said.

He just stared at me, waiting for an explanation.

I stared back. Quite frankly, I didn't want to tell him what I'd done.

"What's wrong with the dog?" he asked. "He looks funny." I was still rubbing Sam's face to no avail. The black wasn't going to wash off.

"I dyed his fur," I mumbled.

The Hubster came over and lifted the towel from the dog's head for a closer look.

"You did WHAT?" he said dropping the towel back over the Wiener.

"He looks like a raccoon!"

"I know he does. What am I going to do?" I wailed. "He has to have his picture taken in three hours."

"Good luck," he said, and "sorry Sam," as he left me to my angst.

So the pictures were taken later that morning.

Sam would not look up.

Sam would not look at me.

Sam was mortified with his new image.

Sam would not even play with his pet brick.

Sam's got a bad dye job.

It really did seem like a great idea at the time.

One short dog short

And now we are one dog short of a full load – a full load being three. (Fortunately, this does not involve a tragedy. It's a good thing, we think.)

It all started when the Hubster called Manchild #2, our 23-year-old guy-kid who recently departed our household to go live in an apartment with friends. His father called to ask him if he would come home and rake the yard. He (the Hubster, not the man-child) indicated there was money involved. When we have a job to hire out, we offer the job to our out-of-work TV guy. (MC2 is a casualty of the Hollywood writers strike despite the fact that he lives in North Charleston and not Hollywood. But even the dark side of S.C. has been affected by the writers strike that has shut down production of the locally shot Lifetime TV series "Army Wives.")

So, MC2 came over with a friend and they worked like crazy people raking the shin-deep layer of leaves that had apparently fallen overnight.

After they finished, we sat around the den chatting when MC2 said he'd been wanting to ask me something for a few weeks.

"Sure. Ask away," I said, a little worried that he wanted his room back.

"I was wondering if I could have one of your dogs. We want a dog real bad. We even called about one, but they'd already given it away. But what we really want is one of yours."

He was serious. And I was dumbfounded. Shocked. But I could see that perhaps he was a little homesick and maybe needed a little touch of home to come live with him.

"You want one of my dogs?" I asked, still getting over the surprise of the request.

"Yes." He was serious. He looked at me steadily and sincerely.

"You can't have Sally, of course, since Sally is MY dog, and you can't have Charlotte because Sally thinks Charlotte as HER dog. Who would she bathe every night if Charlotte was gone?"

(Sally licked Charlotte half to death every night: ears, eyes, top of her head, down to the inside of Charlotte's mouth. Charlotte's got the cleanest teeth in town.)

"What about Cassie?" he asked, looking a little desperate.

At that moment Cassie was sitting on the ottoman next to him and licking his face and – I kid you not – smiling. The dog was practically giggling. She's a very pleasant dog anyway, but she was particularly happy that our youngest guy-kid was in the house. She and he had always been friends. At that point I decided she'd put him up to it.

I looked at Cassie. I looked at him.

"Okay. On a trial basis. You can try it for a few days, but you have to bring her back to visit and run in the back yard. And if it doesn't work out, you bring her right back home." I felt a little strange – lightheaded. What was I saying?

"I will. I promise."

I didn't like giving a pet away. But for the next half hour I instructed him on her care (which he already knew since he only moved out a couple of months ago), got her leash and carrier, bowl, food and blanket. Before I knew it, she was gone.

When the Hubster came home he commented on how clean the patio area was and that the yard looked great.

"Notice anything missing?" I asked.

"Leaves. The leaves are gone." He looked around then asked, "Where's Cassie?"

"With your son."

Later that night my beloved sat on the couch smiling.

"Whatcha' smiling about?" I asked.

"You know what this means, don't you?" the Hubster said wistfully.

"That we only have two dogs and I should go and get another one."

"Wrong. It means our youngest is finally becoming domesticated. He wants something to take care of besides himself."

And that's when I decided it might have been the right thing to do.

Maybe.

Little angels - or monsters?

Our little angels are lying on their sides next to me in the big den chair. They are asleep. They are lined up like cord wood, laid out neatly in a row, their noses peaking over the edge of the chair, their hairy front paws crossed daintily to their sides. They've had their favorite dinner with a teaspoon of pan drippings to sweeten the kibble. It's the way they like it.

They are content.

Sally and Charlotte, the lovely wiener dogs who let us live in their house and sit on their furniture when they aren't using it, need a good brushing.

The reason they need a good brushing is because they have had intermittent displays of insane canine behavior for the last few weeks.

And it all hinges on the doggy door we installed about six months ago.

Let me recap. When first installed, the doggy door was a mystery to them. They were not interested in any door that did not involve us (their pets) getting up to open for them.

But after a few weeks they figured out they could (without our help) go flying out their own personal door into the back yard to chase squirrels whenever the mood struck.

At that point they got over their disdain for the doggy entrance and started using the little swing door on a regular basis.

That has now escalated into what I consider a free-for-all.

It started a few weeks ago. Our domestic engineer a.k.a. manchild, left us a note. The note said the bed was not made because the bed linens were back in the washing machine for the second time that day due to the "two little monsters."

Apparently while the linens were on the floor, they, the angel weenies (a.k.a. "two little monsters") were in the back yard having a digging party looking for God only knows what in a soggy back yard.

While D.E. was changing the bed, the weenies came in their doggy door, jumped into the middle of the clean bedclothes which were lying next to the bed, did the dance of joy all over the bedspread and ran back outside again.

The D.E. was pretty well horrified and a little distressed. When they came back in again the D.E. cleaned the doggy diggers up, put out a rug at the doggy door to cut down on future messes and wrote the aforementioned note.

Then this last weekend, the Hubster and I were sitting in the den watching a good movie when Sally the Princess wiener came running in, leaped onto the ottoman and provoked the Hubster to do his own leaping and exclaiming. He grabbed the dog and took her to the kitchen sink, muttering all the way about the dog mess on the sofa and ottoman.

She had twigs, leaves and briars embedded in her soft hair, glued into the fir with glops of mud. I took over and started pulling refuse out of her hair.

Half an hour later I finally had her reasonably clean.

I put her on the floor and about then I heard the doggy door swing and in came Charlotte the Cheerleader wiener. The only thing worse than the mess I had just cleaned up, was the mess that was now tracking well-defined muddy doggy prints over the floor.

I grabbed her in mid-leap as she aimed for the sofa.

I plunged her into the sink and once again pulled yard refuse from the armpits of a wound-up dog.

At that point, I locked their doggy door and sent them to bed.

So now, we are in a quandary.

Doggy door do, or doggy door don't?

Veggie-wiener: 'Where's the romaine?'

We have these dogs. Wiener dogs. Dachshunds. They actually own us. We are their pets. We fight it pretty hard, but as it turns out Sally and Charlotte are way cuter than we are, and so we let them rule our lives.

Our payment for letting them do this to us is their sheer entertainment value. For instance, the latest discussion is over Charlotte, she of the long, red doggy-hair, and her apparent trend towards becoming a vegetarian. I can honestly say I don't know of any other vegetarian dogs, but I do believe we have one in the making. We discovered her veggie-loving ways a couple of months ago when the Hubster was working on a salad and tossed the heel of a piece of romaine to her. (ust for the record, my guy teases the dogs with food-stuff not normally favored by the canine group. He gets a kick out of offering the dogs items that he hopes will make them recoil and run away because he thinks it's funny. Things like pickles and lemons always get a great reaction as soon as they give a sniff – as you can imagine. I think it all started back when we had our first dog and lived in Germany. MacDuff was a lab-setter mix. A big dog that acted a lot like a very young Jerry Lewis – smart and a little ditzy. One day while we were at the market, a man cooking bratwursts on a grill, dropped one of the sausages by accident. MacDuff wanted it in a big way, straining at his leash to get it. The man picked it up with his long fork and tossed it to MacDuff, who took the brat and ate it whole.

It went straight down his gullet.

And as soon as it hit bottom, it came right back up again, untouched, not a tooth mark on it. It had been hot and soon as it hit Mac's stomach, it had bounced right out. Well, we still laugh when we remember MacDuff and the sausage. (After it cooled off, our good dog got his brat and enjoyed it a lot.)

But that got the Hubster to tossing food to our dogs to see what would happen. This particular day he tossed the lettuce to each of them. Sally, a confirmed meat-eater, looked at it sideways and began to back away as if she was watching a snake about to strike.

Charlotte, on the other hand, picked up the end-chunk of cold white lettuce as if to say, "Finally, the salad course." She chomped down on it, practically swallowed it whole, and came back and begged, standing on her hind legs doing a little dance the likes of which we had not seen before. It was as if we were about to hand her the leftovers of a T-bone steak. She whined. She pranced.

We gave her more lettuce.

Sally watched from across the room in disgust, aghast that any self-respecting dog would act that way.

Now anytime we start getting dinner ready, and the lettuce comes out of the refrigerator, she goes a little nuts and dances around until she gets her salad.

Last night the Hubster tried to give Sally a slice of banana. As expected, she looked at him like he was crazy and left the room. Charlotte, when offered the same slice of banana, wagged her tail, took the slice, and ate it. So now, it seems, sweet Charlotte is into fruit.

I can see a time when Sally is eating her kibble with a dollop of chicken-flavored canned dog food on top, next to Charlotte and her Caesar salad with a side of ambrosia, topped by a dollop of whipped cream.

Vacation packing still crazy

Tomorrow, the Hubster, our wiener dogs and I will go to the lake for 10 fantastic days. We'll stay in the cabin my father, grandfather and uncles built nearly 60 years ago.

I'll go barefoot, wear no makeup and do nothing to my hair other than corral it with a rubber band.

It'll be great.

But first, we have to get there.

So in order to successfully get our stuff from point A to point B, I jotted down a few items I didn't want to forget.

The quick list is now three pages long and is headed by all the stuff I have to take in order to keep the wieners happy and safe. The doggy list is followed by a similar list for us – the humans.

It is basically the same list I used to make in order to take our guy-kids to the lake.

For instance, back then, the list was headed by suntan lotion – more commonly known to today's enlightened mothers as sunscreen. Sunscreen is still on the list – for us and for the dogs' noses as well.

My once-upon-a-time-list included travel bed, stroller, baby food and kid food in addition to grownup food. There were mounds of diapers and stacks of wipes. The new list includes, wiener dog food and doggy treats instead.

Children's medicine figured prominently on the old list from way back when. Those items have now been replaced by flea medicine, heartworm pills and special canine brushes.

Today's list includes doggy gates to keep them from running away. These are the same barriers formerly known as baby gates.

Back then, years before we had a truck, we usually found ourselves caravanning to the lake in both cars just to be able to haul everything up there.

Now that the kids are gone, and we have a truck, the Hubster has to return to the Lowcountry during the middle of the week for a few workdays.

I told him yesterday, "I'll be taking my car this year."

"There's plenty of room in the truck."

"That's true, but the truck will go home with you and you

aren't abandoning me out in the woods without transportation. And the pontoon boat does not count as emergency transportation."

So tonight, before we go, I'll be at the grocery store, and at the department store, and I'll be digging bathing suits and flip-flops out of the back of the closet and getting the leashes and travel kennel out.

I'll pack paper plates and doggy dishes. I'll check the tags and collars on their necks.

And eventually, off we'll go in separate (but as fully loaded as a giant baked potato) vehicles to commune with nature and each other.

And when we get there, we'll unpack and start reading the books we meant to read sooner, take long walks with the wiener dogs, catch a few fish (I hope), ride in the boat, visit with my sister (who has the good fortune to live at her house on the lake), ask friends and family to join us for Memorial Day and just have fun being.

Dog lady still loves those cats

Once upon a time I was a cat person. Not in the same vein as Catwoman (don't I wish), nor even in the same way as the stereotypical recluse with a dozen cats.

But I did, and still do, have an abiding love for felines. (We had to convert to an all-dog household when I found out the reason I was sick all the time was because I was allergic to cats. So, I chose dogs that were as close to cat-like as I could: short and agile dachshunds.)

But still, I love cats. Their independent spirit is appealing; their aloof nature is not all that mysterious to me. Cats are cool. They aren't particularly dependent. Basically, they don't need us.

Take Heather, for instance. Heather was a cat I adopted from a shelter many years ago. When the Hubster and I moved to Germany while he was in the Air Force, Heather stayed with my parents.

So, when they went to Lake Wateree for the annual family vacation, Heather went with them. Heather liked to roam through the woods and scout the lake's edge for a ripe dead fish to roll around on. (Dogs don't have a monopoly on that activity.)

But several weeks later, when it was time to pack up and go back into town, Heather was no place to be found. Momma and Daddy called and called, but Heather didn't show. They went back up looking for her every day for a couple of days, then weeks, and finally decided she was gone for good.

Several months later, my sister Janice went by the cabin to drop something off. By then it was fall, and the place had been empty since the vacation stint. When she got out of the car, Heather came running from the woods, crunching through the fallen leaves, meowing in a very angry tone, obviously quite put out at having been neglected for so long.

She was skinny and irritated, but other than that she was perfectly fine. She had managed on her own all that time. But Heather never strayed away from home again.

The next year when family vacation time rolled around and they moved to the lake, she never left the property. She was always in sight.

This is the same cat that, when she was very young, scared the living daylights out of me one afternoon. I was talking to the future Hubster on the phone. I was in the apartment alone, except for Heather.

As my guy and I chatted away (at the time he was at George Air Force Base in California and I was in Asheville, N.C.), the hallway toilet flushed. It took a second for the impact of that sound to register with me. And then I got very quiet.

I want you to imagine: I'm there alone and the toilet flushes in another part of the apartment. How many things can that mean?

I freaked out, the Hubster-to-be freaked out, and I crept down the hall carrying the metal vacuum cleaner tube as a weapon, only to find Heather walking jauntily out of the bathroom. All I could figure was she had been sitting on the back of the toilet and stepped on the handle on her way down. By then I had searched, and there wasn't anyone else in the apartment, and the place wasn't old enough to be haunted.

This is the same cat that used to get into the cabinets and find personal items she would then drag through the apartment when, and only when, I had company.

This is the same cat, that when I went to the pound (as shelters were known back then) in search of a kitten, had tried with every ounce of strength in her pretty little kitten body to get out of the cage. She had fervently and relentlessly cried and climbed, making as much eye contact as she could, desperate to get her intelligent little self out of there.

How could I not have taken her home?

She was a terrific companion for many years. How diminished our lives would have been without her.

And how different cats are from dogs – even short little agile dogs who love you to distraction.

There's nothing quite as interesting as being a cat's pet.

But to tell you the truth, nothing is more entertaining than a wiener.

She-dogs on hunt in back yard

We have these wiener dogs. Sam, Charlotte and Sally.

Charlotte and Sally are playmates. Sam's the guy, and in true guy form, he just shrugs and walks off when the females in his life start in on whatever they are doing, as long as it doesn't involve one of them eating his food or riding him bareback. In either of those instances, he gets a little testy.

Anyway, the ladies have chosen for their summer entertainment, digging.

They gleefully run out the back door after breakfast, do their morning business and begin nosing around through the grass. They look like diviners, the guys in Westerns who use a divining rod to find water. (I still remember a "Have Gun Will Travel" episode when Paladin is keeping an eye on a stranger who rides into town and says he'll find water for the dusty-looking good folks living there. For some reason, when the diviner walks near an underground water source, the divining rod dips dramatically to the ground to pinpoint the water. The stranger has saved the townspeople because the water will keep their crops from drying up and they won't all starve to death. Loved Paladin, the first celebrity character I remember with just one name.)

Anyway, our dogs look like diviners. Their pointy little noses are the divining rods. (I don't think they are digging for water, however. Fortunately, we don't need them to. We have plenty, especially this summer.)

They continue nosing around in the grass until one of them suddenly goes berserk barking and digging. The other one joins in, and the hunt is on.

For the next hour, they dig nose to nose. Dirt flies out of their hole-in-the-making from between their hind legs. Tails wag frantically in the air as they occasionally come to a screeching halt, stop their efforts and snuffle expectantly into the bowels of the hole. Suddenly, they leap back into their digging frenzy. It is obvious they are on to something, and whatever it is, it has their undivided attention. They are sisters in a quest for what? The great white mole? A snake? We have no idea what they are after.

We, the Hubster and I, are pretty sure of one thing – the "it" is still at-large and living underground in our back yard.

After a long day of digging and barking, they come in at night, snouts covered in a blend of sand and grass clippings that tend to float off their faces into the bottom of the water bowl.

They have a little dinner, sack out for the night and dream, paws still working in their sleep. Barks are muffled in the memory of the hunt.

We are in hopes they never find what they are looking for. There are three reasons for that.

1. They may actually strike water, and we will be a wet version of "The Beverly Hillbillies."

2. We are having way too much fun watching them search.

3. We have watched the movie "Tremors" way too many times and are concerned they will come home with Kevin Bacon or, equally bad, one of those sand worms that eats people.

Unleashing some canine memories

When we got our baby weenie, Charlotte, we bought this newfangled leash (at least it was new to us) that had a lead that breaks away into two leads. We could walk two dogs on the same leash instead of two separate leashes, which they kept crisscrossing and getting tangled in.

We hooked Sally to one lead and Charlotte to the other one. Sally took off running, exuberantly forging ahead, oblivious to 3-pound Charlotte alternately dangling and being dragged by her tiny neck, semi-suspended with little legs bicycling the air, trying to locate Mother Earth.

It didn't look cute. In fact, it very much resembled something for which folks should be arrested.

As it turns out, that type of leash works only if both dogs are approximately the same size and temperament. It's now a year later, and we're still waiting for Charlotte to catch up with Sally.

The leash now resides in the crockery bowl that also contains other failed experiments in dog control. We have what I now consider a comprehensive collection of leashes and collars.

Our dogs have love/hate relationships with their collars.

When Sally was little, she hated hers so much she would wiggle it up to her mouth and chew it off. If we made it any tighter, she wouldn't have been able to breathe. So we got her a miniature body harness, and she chewed that off even faster. She didn't want anything to do with it. She was all about freedom.

But then she got bigger and learned that the sound of her dog tag and collar buckle clinking together meant it was time for an outing. She learned to flip over on her back so we could buckle her up.

Among the items in our collection are hot pink leash-and-collar ensembles, bright green combos, a set of navy blue and another of black. There are chewed-up pieces, worn-out pieces and pieces that never even made it to their little necks, like the heavy chain choker collar with spikes on it that for some reason we thought was a good idea after a particularly vexing afternoon trying to walk them. (None of the dogs has ever had that one on. By the time we got it to the house, it just seemed wrong.)

We have several leashes that are obvious duplicates bought on the spur of the moment because we couldn't find the ones we already had, or we went out of town and forgot to take their leashes with us.

The newest addition to our leash collection is a retractable number that allows the dogs to run 20 feet out from us in the field in front of the river cabin or at the beach (if we can find a beach that allows dogs). That one actually required a learning curve to figure out how to stop or retract the lead.

Then there are those pieces of the collection that are relics from loved and gone-but-not-forgotten pets. Like Sweet Mabel, who spent her last year with us. We have the collar that was hanging inches too big around her emaciated neck the day we found her.

Or MacDuff, the lab/setter mix the Hubster and I got two weeks after we married. His worn black leather collar easily would wrap around all our weenies at once. MacDuff was a joy to our souls, and his accouterments still bring sweet memories.

The collars are like the special baby boy clothes and toys in the Do Not Give Away box – talismans with the power to rebuild the sounds, smells and touches of the past on sight. Some day, far in the future, I will look through the crockery bowl collection and find the double lead leash and smile, remembering the day we found out it wasn't a great idea after all.

Santa meets Sally

I'm having children-at-Christmas withdrawal. The Hubster and I have spent the last few years congratulating ourselves on not having to take our kids to the mall to stand in long lines waiting for Santa to listen to their outrageous requests. But there's been a shift.

We see young parents and wistfully comment, "How sweet."

Stored in the back shed of our memories is the night we stood for more than two hours in a line with a hundred other tired parents and their assorted out-of-sorts kids and watched Santa walk away for his 15-minute break. An insurrection nearly ensued when he disappeared into a nearby store. (Though legal, it seemed un-Christmas-like at the time.)

Our babies were 2 and 6 years old, squirming and

whining tired. We told them we'd come back another night. They cried as if we'd told them Santa wasn't real, "But you promised."

My, how times have changed. Sunday night I asked our 6-foot-2 child, "Do you want to go with me to the mall to see Santa Claus?"

"I'm 18, Mom," he said, raising his eyebrows at me in that, "You can't be serious" way.

"Not for you, kiddo ... to take Sally. I'm not that out of touch with reality," I said. "It's pet photos with Santa night at the mall." (I could see him fighting the urge to make some comment about reality, Santa and Sally)

He declined my invitation in favor of boat-related activities with his father.

Sally and I were the first ones there for the 7-to-9 p.m. photo opportunity. Sally was happy. All 8 pounds of her dragged me toward Santa (he's a great Santa, by the way, with real whiskers) who sat patiently as if waiting just for us. There was no line.

Sally got within two feet of him and went berserk, barking like a maniac, which, of course, put Santa off his jolly HO-HO-HO good mood.

"She's getting close to my face," he said, leaning away, as

I plopped her down into his red velvet-clad arms. About then another dog arrived, Princie the poodle, with festive little Christmas bows plopped on her ears.

Sally greeted them with impassioned yelps that echoed through the mall before sitting still just long enough for her photo. Santa looked a tad anxious as the line continued to grow.

We decided (actually, I decided) to visit with the other dogs. Sally demonstrated her keen interest in this part of the event by acting deranged.

Not one other dog in the entire mall – and by then there were about 40 – was barking. Not one. Except Sally. The cats (yes, there were cats) were calm and cool. One feline, Mr. Samuel J. Culpepper, was pouched in a carrier like the kind in which people carry newborn babies. Mr. S.J.C. was content against his owner's chest. His canine sister was a yellow Lab named Hannah Marie. Both waited patiently in line with their owner.

There were well-loved dogs of every description: Bentley the English bulldog, Julius the pound puppy, Holly Noel the Christmas poodle, Petie the West Highland terrier, and Dallas and Emmett, the great Dane puppies whose heads were bigger than my entire dog.

I'm not sure which is less festive, a whining child or a barking dog. But with a child, someday he or she will grow up and not find a visit with Santa very entertaining.

With a dog, well, she will always be a little dog and in Sally's case, will probably always be excited.

I wonder if Santa will re-up for this gig again next year.

Barking gets more attention

When Sally was a 1-year-old weenie dog, I wistfully took her to the vet to be spayed. Once the deed was done, she came home and slept for the rest of the day.

Day Two she was fine, but by Day Three, Sally was belligerent - not a happy camper. She was angry with us, barking at brother Sam and sister Mabel and rummaging around in the back of my closet.

"That's new," I said to the Hubster as he and I stood there watching her root around in the dark corner, whining. Every now and again she would run out, look at us with a wild-eyed stare, then run back into the shadows, yelping noises that sounded like a squeaky refrigerator door: rubber grinding on rubber.

"What do you suppose that's about?" I asked him.

"She sounds possessed," he replied. I half-expected her

head to start spinning like a canine version of the girl in "The Exorcist." We gathered her from the closet and cuddled her. She barked at us.

By Day Four, Sally developed a swollen belly. She wouldn't eat, wouldn't drink. But she had no fever.

Day Five, I dressed her in her pink collar and leash and hauled her back to the vet.

In the examination room, she barked, acted crazy. I cuddled and consoled her. Then I noticed a framed poem, "The Rainbow Bridge," hanging above the stainless-steel table. The poem described the passage of owners and their pets as they cross the bridge into heaven together, "never to be separated again."

It made me cry.

I held my too-cute Sally tighter. I was feeling guilty for having her spayed in the first place. I stopped reading the poem before we both became hysterical.

About then the vet arrived. She held a wiggling Sally and loved on her. Sally licked and barked. The vet checked her carefully.

"We're really worried," I shouted over the din of Sally's barking. "But she's very energetic and doesn't seem sick at all. She's just acting weird and now with the swelling ... and she won't eat or drink."

The vet looked at me and said, "I know exactly what's wrong." Sally still was licking Doc's face.

"Sally thinks she's pregnant."

"Pregnant? What are you talking about? She was just spayed."

"Sometimes this happens. It's hormonal – a false pregnancy. She'll probably get over it in a week or two," the vet said, adding that she was concerned Sally wasn't eating or drinking anything.

"We've tried everything," I told her. Apparently we had not tried everything, because the vet advised buying Popsicles for her to lick or 7-Up to drink and to get some really yummy dog food that she couldn't resist ... and we should play ball with her and not pet her too much – it could make her condition worse.

So here we are with a dog that's convinced she's pregnant.

She's still checking out the closets to find a place to have her phantom puppies. She won't go anywhere without her lavender terrycloth baby, which she has taken to sleeping on top of.

The Hubster and our he-children are making over her unbelievably.

As far as I can see, she's getting way more attention and coddling out of her hysterical pregnancy (I still can't believe this is going on.) than I ever did with any of my real pregnancies (although I acted pretty much the same way she's acting - except for the barking).

I wonder if I'm too old to fake it and maybe get a Popsicle out of it.

Discovering the joy of doggie gifts

This is how you become the couple that buys lots of doggy gifts. You are suddenly faced with buying Christmas presents for your children, but what they want is a part for the computer or car, or some other weird piece of hardware that no reasonable person would think of as a present. Their gifts are no longer the kinds of things you can run out in the yard and play with on Christmas morning. Watching Surfer Dude make a hole with the new drill Santa brought just isn't the same.

Since our guy-kids are temporarily out of the toy market (and I do believe it is temporary since guys never completely grow up), we have turned our toy attention elsewhere. We have refocused on the littlest members of our household, the three wieners – our version of the three tenors yelping, howling and whining at the back door to be let in. (The dogs, not the three tenors – don't I wish!)

So when I received this very exciting offer for Personalized PetSongs recently, I plopped the enclosed CD into my computer and fired it up. (Unfortunately, I had to try every hole on the back of my computer to find the one the headphone jack belongs to.) I knew I finally had it in the right place as soon as a rousing rendition of "I have a good dog and Moochie is his name" nearly knocked me out of my chair. Very cute. The PetSongs folks will insert your dog's name instead of Moochie (unless, of course, your dog's name is actually Moochie) into the lyrics.

To receive this lovely compilation of seasonal and other songs suitable for year-round listening, all you have to do is send in the name of your dog, the color of your dog, a description of your dog's personality, with (and this is the most important part) $17.95. That's right. For $17.95 you can get a CD chock-full of six full-length songs that address your dog by name. Likely your canine friend will go insane trying to figure out who is calling him or her in such a musical – and I use that word very loosely – way.

If you're not into vocals, you always can go with the traditional, but somewhat boring, dog sweater.

Now don't get me wrong, there are some really wonderful

canine sweaters out there. I'm looking at one right now in the pages of a very holiday-looking catalog. The sweater is described as being a hand-loomed design. It is $98.

As much as we have started doting on our weenie wonders, I feel pretty safe in saying that none of them will be wearing this elegant offering anytime in the near or far future.

Getting into the swing of the season, the Hubster came home last night with a present for the newest member of the household, Teeny Weenie Sweet Charlotte. It is a leggy terry-cloth doll with squeakers embedded in the hands, feet and belly.

In addition to the dog toy, my beloved also purchased the new tool wished for by our oldest grown guy. The tool didn't get a lot of attention.

The squeaky toy, however, did. We squeaked it and tossed it around the room for a while, giggling and playing with it before we finally wrapped it so the dogs would be surprised on Christmas morning. I can't wait for them to open it so we can play with it some more.

All I need now is a little doggy Christmas background music. And maybe that sweater isn't all that expensive after all.

(So this is how it happens.)

Wieners gone wild

Okay, so it wasn't exactly spring-break-style going wild, but the wieners (how can I say this) fully embraced nature on our recent trip to Lake Wateree. (I say Lake Wateree – but to the folks who have been frolicking up there for the last five or six decades or so, it is known more simply as "the river.")

Anyway, it doesn't take much to get our wiener dogs' interest piqued for a trip. The mere touching of a leash and the emergence of their travel kennel from the garage provokes yelping and barking and running in circles the likes of which are an amazement to observe.

As soon as the kennel door opens, they run in and wait patiently to be transported to some far off land – this time the riverside cabin two hours away.

They ride patiently, never making a sound until we turn

into the bumpy driveway to our destination. They know where they are from the feel of the road and the smell of the air. They start whimpering and whining until they are free from the box and ready for vacation. Vacation for them means enthusiastically sniffing scents they have never smelled before. (Or at least since last year.)

First morning I take them out for a walk. They tug on the leash – I might as well be lassoed to a wild horse – as these 10-pound dogs pull me around the yard. Their sniffers are working it hard. They look as if their bodies are being dragged across the lawn by their noses.

I have to wonder, what are they smelling? From the intensity with which they are pursuing the new scent, they are on the track of something wild, I figure it could be a raccoon, or a snake, or another dog perhaps. They finally take a break from sniffing to do their business. I eventually drag them back to the house.

Later we decide to go fishing from the dock. I am prepared. I remembered the year before when I would leash them to the dock post because Sally has a habit of running away in search of heaven only knows what. I was prepared this time. I had packed the baby gates with me, the ones left over from our years of raising the man-children and trying to keep them corralled in a safe area. I set the gates up, pressed between two of the dock posts creating a nice big playpen for the dogs. I could fish and enjoy the afternoon and so could they.

But fishing from the dock seemed a little slow, so I decided to get in the water and wade out from the dock. The dogs watched, curiously sniffing the air.

And that seemed to be going just fine until I heard a splash. In came the once lame, then operated on and rehabbed Sally. I made my way back over to her as she plowed through the water. Her nose held high as she sniffed something in the air and seemed more than a little bit determined to head across the lake. I eventually turned her body around but her head was still yearning for the other direction.

Day after day she jumped off the dock and headed for deep water. We couldn't imagine where she was planning to go, but it was a persistent dream.

Charlotte spent most of her vacation porch-sitting and watching a Carolina Wren build a nest under the house. The little bird picked bits and pieces of sticks and straw from the yard and returned them to her new home site under the edge of the house. It was like observing a dog watching a tennis match: Ears at attention, head swiveling back and forth, back and forth. And sniffing. Always sniffing.

And on the return home, as we released them from their kennel, they frolicked and were just as happy – although the sniffing wasn't half as good – as they had been at the lake.

Because…they're happy little wiener dogs who sniff and frolic wherever they're planted – for a day, a week or a lifetime.

Gotta love'em.

"Living with wieners …and Guys, too" is the first in a series of books by Judy S. Watts. Her second book, "Living with Manchildren…and the Hubster, too" will be released in the fall of 2014.